AMERICA'S INDUSTRIAL SOCIETY IN THE 19TH CENTURY™

The Interstate Commerce Act

The Government Takes Control of Trade Between States

Holly Cefrey

ROSEN CLASSROOM
PRIMARY SOURCE™
Rosen Classroom Books & Materials™
New York

Published in 2004 by The Rosen Publishing Group, Inc.
29 East 21st Street, New York, NY 10010

First Edition

Library of Congress Cataloging-in-Publication Data

Cefrey, Holly.
The Interstate Commerce Act : the government takes control of trade between states/by Holly Cefrey.—1st ed.
v. cm.—(America's industrial society in the 19th century)
Includes bibliographical references and index.
Contents: The need for commerce laws—American frontiers—Interstate commerce—Commerce monopoly—Interstate Commerce Act.
ISBN 0-8239-4027-6 (library binding)
ISBN 0-8239-4282-1 (paperback)
6-pack ISBN 0-8239-4294-5
1. United States. Interstate Commerce Act—History—Juvenile literature. 2. Interstate commerce—Law and legislation—United States—History—Juvenile literature. [1. United States. Interstate Commerce Act. 2. Interstate commerce.]
I. Title. II. Series.
KF2276.53.C44 2004
343.73'088—dc21

2002153698

Manufactured in the United States of America

On the cover: first row (from left to right): steamship docked at a landing; Tammany Hall on election night, 1859; map showing U.S. railroad routes in 1883 (also shown enlarged); detail of bank note, 1822, Bank of the Commonwealth of Kentucky; People's Populist Party Convention at Columbus, Nebraska, 1890; Republican ticket, 1865. Second row (from left to right): William McKinley gives a campaign speech in 1896; parade banner of the Veterans of the Haymarket Riot; Alexander Graham Bell's sketch of the telephone, c. 1876; public declaration of the government's ability to crush monopolies; city planners' illustration of Stockton, California; railroad construction camp, Nebraska, 1889.

Photo credits: cover, p. 19 © Library of Congress, Geography and Maps Division; pp. 6, 10 © Library of Congress, Prints and Photographs Division; pp. 8, 21 © Library of Congress, Rare Books and Special Collections Division; p. 12 © Joseph Sohm, Visions of America/Corbis; pp. 15, 23 © Corbis; p. 25 © DN-004558, *Chicago Daily News* Negatives Collection, Chicago Historical Society; p. 26 Courtesy of the House of Representatives.

Designer: Tahara Hasan; **Editor:** Mark Beyer

Contents

1 The Need for Commerce Laws

Millions of Americans take part in commerce every day by buying, selling, and using products. You take part in commerce. The books that you read and the notebooks that you write in are part of commerce. The clothes that you wear and most things around you are part of commerce.

Service is also a part of commerce. Services include transportation and communication. Companies that own planes, trains, and buses are paid to provide transportation services. Telephone and cable television companies are paid to provide communication services.

We have laws that control how commerce works in business and for consumers. These laws protect us from commerce problems. Goods and services are not always perfect. Companies may not provide safe products or good services. Sometimes books fall apart, buses break

down, and people are cheated. Commerce laws protect people and businesses from harmful products and business practices. Our main set of commerce laws is known as the Interstate Commerce Act. The original act was passed in 1887. Many other commerce laws have been added to the act since 1887. Many of these laws are still used today.

The Trading Post

Native Americans were expert animal trappers. They also had many trails throughout the wilderness, which later became American roads.

In 1795, Congress approved a plan to build fur-trading posts in the western wilderness. The American government built fur-trading posts in the South and the West. These posts were called factories. The factories were stocked with goods. People were hired to trade or buy, store, and ship furs that were provided by the Native Americans. Cities such as Chicago, St. Louis, Albany, and Detroit grew quickly. Fur factories and posts operated there during the 1700s and 1800s.

172 HARPER'S WEEKLY. [APRIL 1, 1876.

Trader's Store.

En Route.

Preparing for Trade.

The Trading Post and Fort

This 1876 woodcut shows how Native Americans used the local trading post. *Clockwise, from upper left:* the trader's store is housed near trails; Native Americans travel to a trading post; they prepare to trade their goods for store goods; the trading post and nearby fort.

People came to America from England and other parts of Europe because of commerce. English and European companies began building trading posts in America in the late 1500s. America offered many resources, such as lumber, land, and animal furs.

People came to trading posts to buy and sell goods. Sometimes people used money to buy goods. Mostly they bartered, or traded, one good for another. Services could also be traded for goods or other services. These might include taking a load of corn down a river to a trading post. This service might cost a bushel of that corn. This was how early business worked in America. Native Americans traded furs for goods such as tobacco, corn, or guns. Traders shipped the furs and other goods back to their countries to sell.

The trading posts grew into colonies as more people came. Eventually, there were thirteen colonies in the easternmost part of America. Many colonists made money by importing or exporting goods. They imported goods from distant lands. They exported goods to foreign countries. They also traded between their different colonies.

England controlled the colonies during the early and middle 1700s. The settlers were English subjects. They paid English taxes. They followed English laws. England

could not control the colonies from overseas. Small units of government were formed in each of the colonies.

Many colonists wanted freedom from England. Local colonial leaders held meetings. In 1776, the colonies

This map was made in 1791. It shows the thirteen states of the United States. Maps show important information used by merchants and other traders. These include cities, major roads, and borders between states. Notice that lands west of the states are named. The United States government had early plans to expand. Trade was very important to the new country.

declared independence from England. England did not want to let go of the colonies. The American War of Independence started a year later. The colonial leaders made an official agreement. The agreement was called the Articles of Confederation. A confederation is a union. The agreement outlined a new government for America.

The Articles of Confederation brought all of the colonies together. The union of colonies called themselves the United States of America. Each colony became a state. Each state had its own government. Each state government could make its own money or coins. The state governments were ordered to be friendly with each other. Each state was

The Mayflower Compact was signed by English settlers in 1620. The document spelled out rules by which the pilgrims would live among each other. When they landed in what is today Massachusetts, they already had laws by which to trade.

free to do commerce with each other. The states were also free to do commerce with foreign governments. The need for commerce laws in the new country became more important.

2
Interstate Commerce

The War of Independence ended in 1783. The colonists were officially freed from England. The states had new, individual governments. This led to problems between the states.

A state government could make whatever laws it wanted. It could charge fees and taxes on goods and business deals. It could control the commerce that took place within its borders. A state government could decide to do business with one state and not another. It could also declare that its money was worth more than another state's money.

America needed a new government. All of the states needed to work together instead of separately. This would make business easier between the states. Business between the states is called interstate commerce.

American leaders wrote the Constitution of the United States in 1787. It became official in 1788. The Constitution

We the People of the United States, in Order to form a more perfect Union, establish Justice, insure domestic Tranquility, provide for the common defence, promote the general Welfare, and secure the Blessings of Liberty to ourselves and our Posterity, do ordain and establish this Constitution for the United States of America.

Article I

Article II

Article III

Article IV

Article V

Article VI

Article VII

done in Convention by the Unanimous Consent of the States present the Seventeenth Day of September in the Year of our Lord one thousand seven hundred and Eighty seven and of the Independance of the United States of America the Twelfth In witness whereof We have hereunto subscribed our Names.

ARTICLE II—EXECUTIVE DEPARTMENT: ... ARTICLE III—JUDICIAL DEPARTMENT: ... ARTICLE IV—THE STATES AND THE FEDERAL GOVERNMENT: ... ARTICLE V—METHOD OF AMENDMENT. Article VI—PUBLIC DEBT; SUPREMACY OF THE CONSTITUTION; OATH OF OFFICE, no religious test required. ARTICLE VII—RATIFICATION OF THE CONSTITUTION.

gave power to a federal, or main, government. Each state would have a smaller government that worked with the federal government. The federal Congress had lawmaking powers. Congress had power over all interstate commerce. The states had to honor all commerce laws made by Congress.

The Constitution settled many early interstate commerce problems. For example, no state could charge a tax or fee for sending goods to another state. Ships traveling from one state to another could not be charged a fee for doing so. Also, only one kind of money would be used throughout the nation. Before this law, each state had its own money. That made commerce troublesome. Congress was also in charge of making commerce deals with foreign countries.

During the 1800s, America changed from a group of trading colonies to a busy nation. Many businesses formed because Americans needed many goods. Textile manufacturers provided clothing and fabrics. Publishing companies provided newspapers, books, and journals. Shipping

The U.S. Constitution lays out the powers of the government. The writers and signers of the Constitution saw the need for a strong federal government. The Constitution balanced powers fairly between government branches. States held powers to trade between themselves and foreign governments. Fair trade was an important part of constitutional control over states.

companies provided new boats and transportation. Farming communities supplied food and livestock. All these goods needed to be shipped between the different states.

Suddenly, interstate commerce became hard for Congress to control. Congress made a board, or committee, to help with commerce responsibilities. The Committee on Commerce and Manufacturers began in 1816. The committee focused on making roads, canals, and rivers better for travel. It understood that interstate commerce could run more smoothly if travel was easier and safer. The committee made harbor improvements where ships docked for

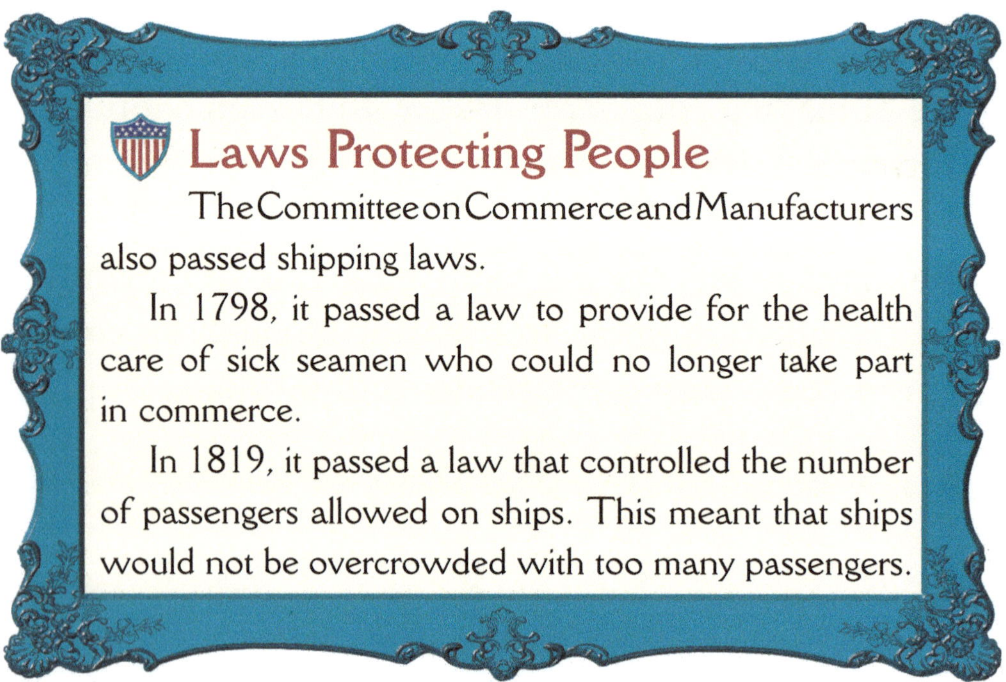

Laws Protecting People

The Committee on Commerce and Manufacturers also passed shipping laws.

In 1798, it passed a law to provide for the health care of sick seamen who could no longer take part in commerce.

In 1819, it passed a law that controlled the number of passengers allowed on ships. This meant that ships would not be overcrowded with too many passengers.

The steamship *William Corig* carried cotton bales down the Mississippi River. Trade ports along the river allowed the ship to stop and pick up more cargo. The ship would be full by the time it reached New Orleans. Safe harbors, trade routes, and fair prices helped U.S. agriculture prosper in the nineteenth century.

trade. It also decided where ports should be built.

In 1825, the committee divided itself in two. It became the Committee on Manufacturers and the Committee on Commerce. Now each could focus on the job of either

manufacturing or selling. The Committee on Commerce made more laws that governed shipping and commerce. For example, commerce ships had to be registered with the government. This helped keep track of goods and commerce. Americans began using steam-powered ships during the middle 1800s. Many early steam boilers exploded. The committee made laws to make steamship travel safer.

3
Commerce Monopoly

Railroad tracks were laid throughout the eastern United States beginning in the early 1840s. Train service helped interstate commerce. Many goods could be shipped easier and farther on trains than on river or road routes. Railroad companies also offered passenger service. Many companies offered local service within each state. This allowed small towns to grow into busy cities.

American citizens, businesses, and farmers used trains a great deal. Railroad company owners became very wealthy. They charged whatever they wanted for their services.

Some cities and towns had only one railroad company that provided service. Many companies charged high prices if they were the only railroad in town. They held a monopoly on service because no other company could offer services. When a company acted as a monopoly, it was in complete and unfair control. Passengers had to pay

Taming the West

Much of western America was still wilderness when rail tracks were laid in the West. Congress passed the Homestead Act in 1862. This law helped to settle the wild western part of America. Settlers were given 160 acres of free western land. In exchange, the settler had to live there for five years and improve the land. Soon new towns, cities, and states formed in the West.

high prices in order to use the service because it was the only service available.

Many American companies had commerce monopolies. For example, Ira Munn had a monopoly on grain in Chicago. Munn was a businessman who invented grain elevators. These were large storage bins for grain. He built them along railroad lines and the Chicago River. When farmers sent their grain, it was stored in Munn's bins. Munn stored the grain until prices were high and then sold the grain. Many grain merchants like Munn cheated farmers. Farmers were not paid the full worth of

Railroad construction blossomed through the mid-1800s. By the 1880s, more than 150,000 miles of track had been laid or were planned. Railroad transportation became the fastest and most economical way to travel and trade by the end of the nineteenth century.

the grain they shipped to merchants. Some farmers were also charged taxes for grain storage.

Farmers were also unhappy with the railroads. Railroad owners were charging so much that it was too expensive to send grain and other goods. Many trains would

Granger Laws Help Farmers

The court case of Munn v. Illinois is also known as a Granger case. "Granger" is an old name for farmers, who started the movement. They took the name from the National Grange of the Patrons of Husbandry. In 1867, the farmers banded together to fight unfair commerce. They asked political leaders to make laws to control monopolies and unfair commerce. The laws—like the ones made by Illinois and Wisconsin—became known as Granger laws. Court cases that fought the laws were called Granger cases.

not arrive on time. State governments, such as those in Illinois and Wisconsin, decided to stop grain merchants and railroad owners from taking advantage of their states' farmers. They passed laws to control rates and stop unfair merchant activities.

Ira Munn fought the Illinois law against merchant activities. He said that he could charge what he wanted because he was providing a service. He felt he could do what he wanted because the bins were on his privately owned land.

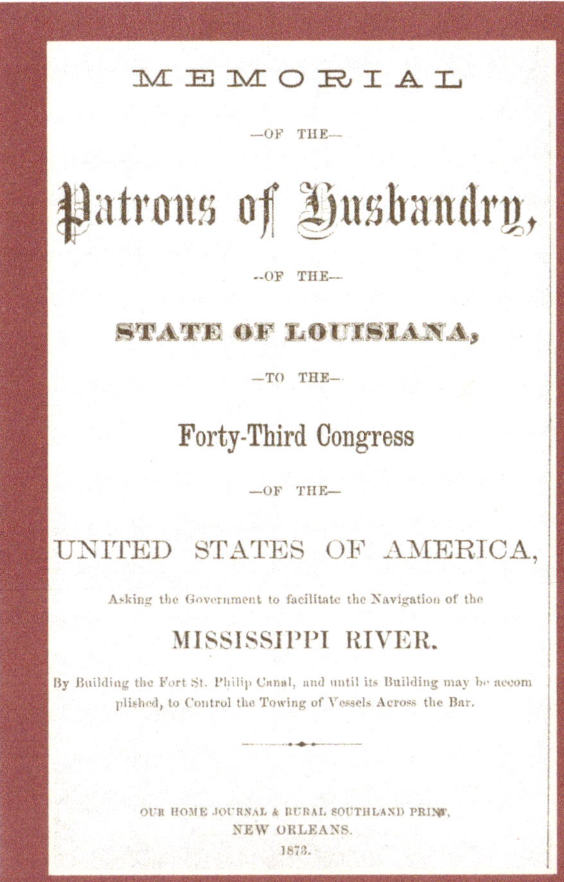
MEMORIAL

—OF THE—

Patrons of Husbandry,

--OF THE--

STATE OF LOUISIANA,

—TO THE—

Forty-Third Congress

—OF THE—

UNITED STATES OF AMERICA,

Asking the Government to facilitate the Navigation of the

MISSISSIPPI RIVER.

By Building the Fort St. Philip Canal, and until its Building may be accomplished, to Control the Towing of Vessels Across the Bar.

OUR HOME JOURNAL & RURAL SOUTHLAND PRINT,
NEW ORLEANS.
1873.

The Patrons of Husbandry was a group of Louisiana farmers. They formed to protect their trade rights. They demanded that laws be passed protecting safe river passage for their produce. Many such husbandry groups formed throughout the United States in the late nineteenth century. State governments began to pass laws protecting trade within their own states.

The Supreme Court ruled against Munn in 1877. The Court decided that a state government had a right to control any commercial activity. The state could control any commerce that affected the public, even if it was done on private land. This was an important decision. Soon other states made similar commerce laws.

4
The Interstate Commerce Act Becomes Law

Unfair commerce continued even after many states made commerce laws. It was difficult for state governments to control each and every commerce activity. The laws varied from state to state. Also, the laws could not cover every issue of commerce.

The public wanted fair commerce throughout all America. They wanted laws that all companies had to follow. They wanted lower fares. They wanted lower taxes and reliable goods and services.

Senator Shelby Cullom of Illinois was put in charge of a special committee. The committee reported on transportation activities involved in commerce. Senator Cullom wrote a report and gave it to Congress on January 18, 1886. He suggested a law be made to enact commerce laws. Congress decided to make an official

Illinois senator Shelby Cullom ran a government committee to establish national commerce laws. The Interstate Commerce Commission was established to oversee and enact Interstate Commerce Act laws. Fair trade, reasonable costs, and controlling big business became the heart of the commission and the act.

set of commerce laws. This resulted in the Interstate Commerce Act.

The Interstate Commerce Act gave power over commerce to a new committee. This was the Interstate Commerce Commission, or the ICC. It had five members called commissioners.

The ICC was in charge of controlling transportation companies that took part in interstate and foreign commerce within the United States. These transportation companies included railroads and shipping lines. The ICC also controlled companies that provided water, oil, and shipping or delivery services.

The ICC made new rules according to the act. The ICC investigated complaints about unfair commerce. Railroad

The Interstate Commerce Act—February 4, 1887

The act included the following laws about railroad companies:

- Rates and fares had to be published for all to see.
- Companies could make only reasonable increases to their published rates.
- Companies were not allowed to give individual discounts to customers such as shipping companies.
- Companies were not allowed to show favor to one city over another.
- Companies were not allowed to show favor to one kind of shipment over another (for example, favoring shipping of textiles over grain).
- Short trips could not cost more than long trips.

companies were ordered to give yearly reports to the ICC. The reports listed rates and practices. High and unfair rates were not allowed.

For the first ten years, the ICC tried to enforce the Interstate Commerce Act laws. It held many sessions to investigate commerce complaints. Unfortunately, the ICC

Members of the Interstate Commerce Commission met to hear commerce complaints. Businesses around the country sought their help in disputes. The ICC had few enforcement powers, however. By the early 1900s, more laws were needed to control unfair business practices.

did not have the power to punish lawbreakers. The commissioners had to build a case against a company. The company had to be taken to court. The court decided if the company was guilty. A court could rule against the ICC's case.

This process was frustrating to the ICC commissioners. The ICC reported in 1897 that "the people should no longer look to [the ICC] for protection" because the ICC was powerless. In fifteen cases, the Supreme Court ruled against the ICC's decisions about unfair railroad activities.

During the early 1900s, more laws were added to the Interstate Commerce Act. The Elkins Act of 1903 and the Hepburn Act of 1906 gave more power to the govern-

[Public No. 41.]

Forty-Ninth Congress of the United States of America;

At the Second Session,

Begun and held at the City of Washington on Monday, the sixth day of December, one thousand eight hundred and eighty-six

AN ACT

To regulate commerce.

Be it enacted *by the Senate and House of Representatives of the United States of America in Congress assembled,* *That* the provisions of this act shall apply to any common carrier or carriers engaged in the transportation of passengers or property wholly by railroad, or partly by railroad and partly by water when both are used, under a common control, management, or arrangement, for a continuous carriage or shipment, from one State or Territory of the United States or the District of Columbia, to any other State or Territory of the United States, or the District of Columbia, or from any place in the United States to an adjacent foreign country, or from any place in the United States through a foreign country to any other place in the United States, and also to the transportation in like manner of property shipped from any place in the United States to a foreign country and carried from such place to a port of transshipment, or shipped from a foreign country to any place in the United States and carried to such place from a port of entry either in the United States or an adjacent foreign country: Provided, however, That the provisions of this act shall not apply to the transportation of passengers or property, or to the receiving, delivering, storage, or handling of property, wholly within one State, and not shipped to or from a foreign country from or to any State or Territory as aforesaid.

The term "railroad" as used in this act shall include all bridges and ferries used or operated in connection with any railroad, and also all the road in use by any corporation operating a railroad, whether owned or operated under a contract, agreement, or lease; and the term "transportation" shall include all instrumentalities of shipment or carriage.

All charges made for any service rendered or to be rendered in the transportation of passengers or property as aforesaid, or in connection there

On February 4, 1887, the Interstate Commerce Act established national control over trade between the states. The most successful part of the act was forcing the railroads to charge fair prices for the transportation of grain from farms to urban markets.

ment and ICC over railroads. By 1917, the ICC was able to bring the railroad industry under control. Passengers were charged fair rates. Train service became safer and more dependable. Commerce ran more smoothly because strict rules prevented railroad companies from taking advantage or becoming monopolies.

New commerce was introduced to America during the late 1800s and early 1900s. For example, telephones, radios, and motion pictures were new businesses. At first, problems with new commerce were brought to the ICC. The government decided to make new committees to help control growing commerce. State governments also made smaller committees for local control. Slowly the ICC's power was taken away and given to new committees.

Today, the ICC no longer exists. The government stopped the commission's work on December 29, 1995. The ICC Termination Act was passed. The very last of the commission's duties were given to the Surface Transportation Board of the Department of Transportation. These duties involved the control of rates and routes of railroads and trucking services. The ICC's other laws have also been taken over by other government agencies. Though the ICC no longer looks after interstate commerce, people and laws are always on the lookout to protect business and consumer needs.

Glossary

commerce (KAH-mers) The buying and selling of goods and services to make money.

Congress (KON-gres) The government body that makes laws.

enforce (en-FORS) To make sure that a law is obeyed.

interstate commerce (in-ter-STAYT KAH-mers) The buying and selling of goods and services to make money between states.

manufacture (man-yuh-FAK-cher) To make something, often by using machines.

monopoly (muh-NAH-puh-lee) The complete control of a product or service for sale to the community.

product (PRAH-duhkt) Something that is made or manufactured.

regulate (REH-gyoo-layt) To control or manage.

resource (REE-sors) Something valuable or useful to a place or person.

Web Sites

Due to the changing nature of Internet links, the Rosen Publishing Group, Inc., has developed an online list of Web sites related to the subject of this book. This site is updated regularly. Please use this link to access the list:

http://www.rosenlinks.com/aistc/inca

Primary Source Image List

Page 6: Woodcut from drawings by W. M. Cary in *Harper's Weekly*, 1876. It is currently housed at the Library of Congress in Washington, D.C.

Page 8: 1791 map of the United States with adjoining provinces. It is currently housed at the Filson Historical Society, Louisville, Kentucky.

Page 10: Photograph made between 1910 and 1930 of a painting showing the signing of the Mayflower Compact. It is currently housed at the Library of Congress in Washington, D.C.

Page 12: The United States Constitution, 1789. It is currently housed at the National Archives in Washington, D.C.

Page 15: Nineteenth-century photo of the steamboat *William Carig* loaded with cotton.

Page 19: 1882 railroad map of railroads under construction. It is currently housed at the Library of Congress in Washington, D.C.

Page 21: Cover of the pamphlet titled *Memorial of the Patrons of Husbandry of the State of Louisiana*, 1873. It is currently housed at the Library of Congress in Washington, D.C.

Page 23: Nineteenth-century photograph of Senator Shelby Cullom.

Page 25: 1907 photo of Interstate Commerce Commission meeting in Chicago, Illinois. It is currently housed at the Library of Congress in Washington, D.C.

Page 26: The Interstate Commerce Act, 1887. It is currently housed at the National Archives in Washington, D.C.

Index

About the Author

Holly Cefrey is a freelance writer. Her books have been placed on the Voice of Youth Advocates National Nonfiction Honor List. She is a member of the Authors Guild and the Society for Children's Book Writers and Illustrators.